Blessed Along the Way

By William S. Davies

Rome, Georgia

Copyright © 2020 by William S. Davies
All rights reserved.

Special thanks to Dr. Ross West, Martha Heneisen, Cathy Aiken-Freeman, and my wife Merrill for assisting in getting these stories ready for publication.

The frog icon: I grew up in a community called Frog Level, and my wife's high school mascot was the bullfrog!

*Additional copies of this book may be found at Amazon.com.

Table of Contents

Preface 7

Biographical Tales 9
Coming to America 11
Land of the Free and Plenty 12
Up the Road a Piece 13
Letter to Elias 16
Llanwanno 18
Edwin's Harp 20
The Great Flood 23
Harlan Train 26
Detroit Cold 28
Detroit Diaspora 30
Turkey Creek and Aunt Kittie 32
Mexico 34
John Sparks Johnson 36
A License to Drive 38
Last Words 41
Another Bill 45

Church Tales 47
Baptizing at the Brickyard 49
Funeral: It's Not What You Thought. 51
Leonard Filardo 53

Misunderstood	55
Hope for Healing	58
We Don't Know You!	60

Hunger and Homelessness   63
Abandoned	65
A Meal on the Way to Hell	67
Archie	69
Asher	70
Worth Saving	72
Feet Hurt	76
Luke	77
Ichabod	79
Kilion: Help Me Get a Job	81
Lazarus	82
Porch Guest	84
Walking in the Fog	85
Steve	90
Tapping	94
A tribute to Tattoos	95
Whose Table Is This Anyway?	97

Strange   **99**
Hoot	101

Chester	102
Denver Dog	103
Don't Look	104
Elevator	105
Ham in Court	108
Sisters	110
Real Law	111
Naked and Dead	113
Names	115
Norman	116
Pilgrim	118
Resurrection	120
Right or Wrong, Heaven or Hell	122
Slick	123

Preface

Frederick Buechner says, "In the biblical sense, if you give me your blessing, you irreversibly convey into my life not just something of the beneficent power and vitality of who you are but something also of the life-giving power of God, in whose name the blessing is given."

God, family, church, community and friends have blessed my pilgrimage. True blessing demands that it be shared. Each of these stories in some way is a thread in the fabric of my life.

It has been over fifty years since some of these events happened. Time and the retelling of them may have modified the borders of truth.

Some of us were born and grew up just before television. We were nurtured by a generation that lived in a world of stories. The exchange of stories was a regular and frequent part of the daily commerce.

Story appreciation is inborn and as natural as breathing. It is part of my DNA. From the time I was an infant, stories were told at home, Dad's store, church, school, and in the community. They affected world view. My mother, father, brother, wife, aunts, uncles and cousins constantly reinforced the oral tradition.

My faith journey has been formed through these stories. Myron Madden's *The Power to Bless* speaks plainly that we have all been blessed and all share in the blessing of others. May these stories in some way bless you.

Biographical Tales

Coming to America

In Wales I stood outside your front door
    And walked inside on your floor.
1903 you walked out into the yard,
    left your home, it must have been hard.
Coming to America.

Mother, brothers, sister, and you,
    doing what you had to do.
With the Irish, Germans and Welsh,
    seeking a place for yourself,
Coming to America.

Edwin, your father, came the year before
    Margaret, your mother, sought the shore.
Children, goods, hopes, and dreams,
    all in baskets it seems,
Coming to America.

Miners from the pits like Treharris,
    And families from the Rhonda
Were filled with hopes, dreams,
    Fears, excitement, and fond of
Coming to America.

Land of the Free and Plenty

From Mountain Ash, Rhondda Valley, New South Wales, Great Britain, Edwin made his way to America. His cousins had already arrived and established themselves as coal miners in the community of Princeton, Kentucky.

Such was the migration of the Davies clan during the last decade of the nineteenth century and the first decade of the twentieth century. Dreams were many, and hopes were high. The following fills in the blanks of what might have happened.

Years ago someone in the family told me how Edwin was welcomed into the home in Kentucky.

Edwin inquired at the train station and located the family home of his cousins. The hills looked the same as those in Mountain Ash, Wales. He was received with great joy. Written correspondence for months had anticipated his arrival, and the celebration would be appropriate.

They talked. The noise in the kitchen suggested much preparation. Having eaten only what he could purchase or what was in his bag on the way, a real meal sounded wonderful.

Escorted into the kitchen/dining room to a carefully prepared table, Edwin noticed there was no meat, only plentiful bread and greens, every kind of greens you could imagine. Being the honored guest, Edwin was asked to offer the blessing. The result was, "Lord, we thank you for this land of the free and plenty, where we eat grass like a damn cow. Amen."

Up the Road a Piece

The first time I heard of Elias Lewis Jr. I was too young to care, almost six decades ago. I knew he was out there somewhere. The thought of him has entered my consciousness numerous times. Today I sat at my desk trimming a picture of him. Cousin Mary Gwen found it among Aunt Ellen's pictures. I had assumed that no picture existed in our world.

For her last years until 1947 Margaret lived at 525 Manchester Street, Barbourville, Kentucky. She was the wife of Edwin. Both were immigrants from the coal mining community of Mountain Ash in the Rhondda Valley, South Wales.

Edwin arrived in 1902 at Philadelphia on his way to Kentucky. Margaret and their children—stepson Elias Lewis, Jr.; David, Ellen, and my father, Bill—had arrived in Mountain Ash, Whitley County, southeastern Kentucky in 1903. Margaret was the widow of Elias Lewis, Sr. She then married Edwin Davies.

Margaret was, as most Welsh women, just barely five feet tall. She had a backbone of steel. With Edwin in America, she sold everything they could not carry in their arms or luggage. She dressed, managed, fed, and encouraged her children through Ellis Island. The boys had a rash upon arrival and medical inspection and were assigned to the Ellis Island hospital. She and Ellen stayed until they were released, and all could catch a train to Tennessee.

As a child, Elias Lewis, Jr., had gone to school and studied writing, poetry, and voice. After finishing school he worked with redheaded Billy Walters at his store where his mother did the meat cutting and his father ran the store. When Elias arrived in Kentucky, Edwin got him a job as a "trapper" in the mines, waiting to open doors for miners and coal cars. It lasted only a short time. Elias then found a job as a clerk at the Carmarthen Hotel in Jellico, Tennessee.

I have only three physical pieces of evidence to suggest that Elias ever existed, a note in Ellen's history of the family, a post card, and recently found picture. He loved to travel and went as far as Pennsylvania to visit Aunt Mary and Uncle Evan Powell.

Ellen said the wanderlust got him again. He worked on "tramp" steamships and visited places such as Spain, Italy, England and Egypt. My brother Sam has the postcard, passed down through the family. It is a picture of the pyramids in Egypt. Elias shared only a few words describing the beauty of it.

In 1918 the great flu epidemic killed millions. We think he might have died of the flu and was buried at sea as were thousands of others.

Intellectually Margaret must have known, but a mother's heart had to believe that he was still coming home. I was raised in the house next door. Until her death in 1947 she repeated the ritual of sweeping the walk and watching.

They say she would stop occasionally and linger at the end of the walk. Each time she would, as mountain people say, "look up the road a piece," hoping to see Elias. The porch, walk, street, and road are still there. "Chesed" is the Hebrew word for everlasting love.

Letter to Elias

I am ages past being able to speak with you, Elias. Perhaps writing you a letter would help me at least.

The first time I heard of you, six decades ago, I was too young to care. I knew you were out there somewhere. The thought of you has entered my consciousness numerous times. Today I sat at my desk trimming a picture of you. Cousin Mary Gwen found it among Aunt Ellen's pictures. I assumed that no picture existed in our world.

I sat in Aunt Ellen's living room and heard about your coming to America. Your step-father had come the year before in 1902 followed by you and your mother Margaret, sister Ellen and brothers Dave and Bill (my father). Your brother Ted was born in the U.S. a few years later. Yours was a coal mining family from the Rhondda valley of South Wales, Great Britain.

You were born the son of Elias Lewis and Margaret Simon Lewis (Davies) on Ann Street, Glamorganshire, South Wales. You went to school in Clyfynydd, Pontygwaith, and Taylorstown and were given lessons in writing, poetry, and voice. Upon finishing school, there was work in Billy "Redhead" Walter's store. Grandmother Margaret did the meat cutting and Grandfather Edwin ran the store. Now I know why Bill, my dad, opened a store when he married and left the mines.

Upon arrival in America, you found work in Mountain Ash, Kentucky, as a trapper. Trappers simply waited at each door inside the mines to close them to each leg in case there were fires or explosions. You were older than the other trappers. Many of them started as early as five years of age, sitting and waiting to hear the sound of a rail car on the tracks.

Ellen said the "wanderlust" overcame you. Finding work on boats, you traveled to Italy, Spain and England. My brother has the postcard, passed down through the family. It is a picture of the pyramids in Egypt. You shared only a few words describing the beauty of it.

In 1918 we had the great flu epidemic that killed millions. We think you might have died of the flu and were buried at sea.

Your mother must have known, but a mother's heart had to believe that you were still coming home. I was raised in the house next door. Until her death in 1947 she repeated the ritual of sweeping the front walk and watching.

They say she would stop occasionally and linger at the end of the walk. Each time she would, as mountain people say, "look up the road a piece," hoping to see you. The porch, walk, street, and road are still there. "Chesed" is the Hebrew word for everlasting love.

Blessings,

Bill

Llannwanno

In 1994 I was able to go to the row house where they lived. Llanwanno is exactly as Edwin's daughter, Aunt Ellen, described. She wrote down everything she could remember. Not a single descendent had returned there since Edwin, my grandfather, left in 1902. His wife, Margaret, and children, Bill (my father), Ellen and Dave left in 1903.

We searched for the family home, school, and cemetery. Llanwanno, a farm settlement in the Rhondda Valley, gave its name to the cemetery. (Llanwanno means the *Church of Gwynn*.)

Entering this part of the Rhondda Valley the hills are steep. The stone is everywhere, a white limestone, and any green is grass or crops of gardens covering the terraces. The stone in every house and garden wall, walk, or well is the same, unmoved for decades, centuries.

The home place was a row house on the side of a hill. It was called the "Upper Terrace." "Upper, Middle, and Lower" referred to the three terraces, not a class distinction. There was considerable competition between children of the three terraces.

The row house is just where she said. Every window, door, step and view is as if she had drawn a picture. Ellen said there were seven steps out back. There were nine but the current neighbor said two had been added.

The infant school was on the opposite side of the valley and unchanged in 1994. When we went back in 2000 with my brother, it was completely absent.

This was a mining village. Most mining was coal and some slate. Now pits such as Treharris are closed. Long ago machines had closed the mines and some people have left. Such pits were called "gaseous." Wherever there is coal there is methane. Ellen wrote of the mine explosion that took the lives of a number of family members.

Our guide for the day helped us find the town and the cemetery. It was a typical Welsh cemetery with the limestone fence, green vines, and stone markers. At one corner of the yard was a stone church. We inquired about seeing inside the church. A local cemetery visitor let us know that is was the custom that church keys were available at the pub next door. We inquired and were able to view the inside of a building that was centuries old.

Our guide found the family marker. My great grandmother, Elizabeth Morgan Simon Reece, is buried there. Her husband named William Simon, from whom I take my name, is buried there. Great uncle, Elias Lewis, and three children are named on markers.

We found the marker for which we searched. It had the names of a number of family members. Some were as young as fourteen. All were killed in a mine explosion. Ellen said they would be there. It stood as a memorial to those who had died and also a marker for the many who died in "gaseous" mine explosions over the centuries and around the world. Our family came to America partly because someone said the mines were safer here.

Edwin's Harp

Some things in life have value not because of their physical worth but because of the stories they carry. So it is with Edwin's harp. It was in one corner of the living room in my grandmother's home until she died. My aunt Ellen kept the harp there until her death. My mother, Alice lived there until her death.

Edwin's harp had stood in the corner at 525 Manchester Street from 1919, at the arrival of Edwin, Margaret, Lewis, Dave, Ellen, Bill, and Ted, until it was moved to cousin David's house in Harlan after Ellen's death. I cannot remember anything before being aware of that harp. I never saw anyone play a note on it.

27 Upper Terrace, Stanleytown, Rhondda Valley, South Wales, Great Britain was their home in Wales. The parlor was the first room on the right of the interior passage. It was always closed except on Sundays when they had tea or cakes (pie or fruit) or whenever relatives would visit. Two harps provided the musical entertainment in this parlor. My wife, Merrill, and I visited the row house in the 90s.

There was a fireplace, blackened with lead, and brass, shined each week. An armchair stood on each side of the fireplace. Often they would play in the evening. My great grandfather, David, was known in the community as Dai the harpist. His harp was on the left, and Edwin, my grandfather, kept his harp on the right. Playing sessions were on Sunday afternoons and occasional evenings when relatives visited.

My great grandfather came from Wales to 310, South Main Avenue, Scranton, Pennsylvania, to visit his sister. While there he purchased a third hand, double action, Erad, Delvoaus (French maker) harp. (Aunt Ellen's description.)

Upon return to Wales David began to study under Johnnie Bryan, a student of the Royal Academy of Music in London. He also studied under Dick Price, another highly regarded harpist.

Edwin and Dai played in numerous public venues and during mining strikes found work playing the harps. They would travel with a violinist, a singer, and a dramatist ("action man"), from town to town doing concerts and dances.

I cannot find the written record but Edwin brought the harp to America before the rest of his family arrived. We know he landed at Philadelphia in January of 1902, arriving on the Steamer Majestic of the White Steamship Lines and sought two passenger train tickets to Bowling Green, Barren County, Ky. He was told the harp was freight, and it could not occupy a seat. Thus he rented space in a freight car to Bowling Green, then a boat down the Green River to Coffman, Kentucky (near Princeton) to meet a brother, David. He almost froze to death on the freight car ride.

They were told he could be recognized because he carried the Erad harp in a Kilarney green cloth case over a navy-blue case. While he waited for the boat, he played his harp on the pavement outside the hotel. Many listened, but no one offered a penny as they had in the Rhondda.

Edwin went to work with his relatives in the mines. Often, when the mines were shut down Edwin would travel and find other work. Margaret had the harp painted by a traveling artesian when Edwin was working out of town. I was told that he was greatly displeased upon returning home and finding that his harp had been covered in flowers.

In 2012 my wife, Merrill, and I visited the harp and cousin David in Harlan, Kentucky. David and my brother Sam had already been talking of restoring the harp. Sam and David did some serious investigation.

Aunt Ellen's written family history was the basis of Merrill's novel, *The Welsh Harp*. At a book signing in northern Kentucky, a lady harpist unexpectedly appeared and played in the background during the signing. She had seen notice of the book signing in the community. After the signing we went to the shop where she worked as an assistant restorer of stringed instruments. Later my brother Sam was able to get this music shop to restore the harp.

December 30, 2015, Sam went to Crestwood, Kentucky, to get the harp and return it to his office in Barbourville, Kentucky. Our research tells us it was made in 1825. It is now restored.

The Great Flood

The small city of Barbourville, Kentucky, is located in the Cumberland valley. It is subject to occasional flooding.

By the time the police came to his house, Edwin had found a dry spot. He placed his rocking chair on the dining room table. Beside him was a small end table. Upon it were the following items: candles, matches in a can, one round block of cheese on a plate, crackers, one knife, his pipe, tobacco in a can, a loaded pistol, a large jar of water, a bottle of whiskey and a glass.

"Edwin. You in there?" Here they stood. Two city police deputies, Marvin Hastert and Willie Tuttle. They were fully uniformed, armed and in boots up to their knees. Edwin said, "You know I'm in here or you wouldn't be out there 'hollerin.' Who sent you?"

Marvin responded, "Margaret sent us. She's worried sick about you." Edwin replied, "Tell her I'm fine, take care of the kids. I'll come to where they are as soon as the water's gone."

The house had been there for half a century before this flood arrived. A white frame, one floor house with a bay window in a small Kentucky town was typical of America in the 1930s and 1940s. It was 1933.

There are many advantages of being in a river valley, but occasionally there was a flood. Every five to ten years the flood would come bringing three feet of water into the house.

The deputies waded into the living room. This wasn't their first conversation with Edwin. They knew him as a Welsh immigrant and a coal miner. He came here in 1902 and sent for his wife and children in 1903. He worked his way up to coal mine foreman and owner. He was a proud American, five feet and one-inch-tall, weighed less than a hundred pounds, yet a man to be considered if confronted. His hands and arms showed the coal tattooing of his trade.

Deputy Tuttle asked, "You okay, Edwin?"

He responded, "You can't make me leave. You know the group that lives around here. If I leave today, there will be nothing left here tomorrow!"

Deputy Hastert said, "Tell him we'll keep an eye on it. He needs to leave and stay at Doc's place downtown." Doc was Edwin's son, Ted.

"Leave? No. My sons and I worked the mines with 'bushy eye browed' John L. Lewis. I left twenty of my kin and friends who died in the mine disaster in Llangllolen, South Wales, buried in a common grave. I ain't leavin here."

The deputies continued to plead. Old man Pierce from next door and Jennings from across the street had come to the door and shouted, "Are you in there? Do you need anything to eat or drink?"

He told Pierce, "See that harp on the table over there, I rode a freight car from Philadelphia to Princeton, Kentucky, in the winter of 1902 because they said the harp was freight. They wouldn't sell me a second ticket so it could ride next to me in the passenger car. I am not leaving it now."

Pierce exclaims, "It could take some days for the water to rise and recede."

"I'll wait it out." He sat and rocked until the slicing sound of the rockers and the sloshing of water against the walls stopped.

The deputies returned two more times to no avail. They cussed him each time he would turn them away.

After three days the water went down, and he went to work cleaning up, moving family back in and then back to the mines, like his neighbors. This was the "Great Flood," but not the last.

Harlan Train

I can see it as clearly as if it were yesterday, the train depot. It was one of those train depots that dotted the hills of Appalachia in the 1950s long past its useful life.

The anticipation of going to see Uncle Dave, Aunt Io (named after the Greek goddess Io), and cousin David was almost more that we could bear. I was seven and my brother Sam was five. Uncle Dave was the favorite uncle on my father's side. Tiny, wiry, short and fast moving, he would always box with us. Aunt Io was as tiny and as joyful. They were the perfect pair.

For kids who had not been more than fifty-five miles away from home, this was an absolute delight. In the two or three trips we made, my brother and I stayed awake all night in anticipation. The taxi would come and take us to the depot, and we would wait forever for the train.

It was a delightful ride, two or three passenger cars attached to the end of a coal train. The soot was everywhere. It was summer and hot. The windows were partially down to keep air moving even if the coal dust got all over us. The conductor came through every few minutes announcing "Artemus, Kay Jay, Blackmont, and Harlan."

Leaving home before daylight and following the crooked tracks through the deep valleys, we could almost see through the fog. Most of the year, the sun came up mid-morning and went down far too early in the late afternoon.

Through the train windows we could see the mountains, streams, trees and people. It was long before strip mining. It was years before the trees were clear cut.

The depot is gone. The train no longer has passenger cars. The conductor is silent. Uncle Dave and Aunt Io are gone and I cannot return to them. The memories are still alive in conversations with their son David and others in our family.

Detroit Cold

In February of 1958, Detroit was cold, knee deep in snow, and the wind was howling, The Yellow Cab let us out at the front of Uncle Andy's boarding house, a brownstone apartment building in the dying light downtown on National. My mother, my eleven-year-old brother, and I (age thirteen) were glad to be at our destination.

All my life I had heard of it, the great city of the Southern diaspora. Some in our community went to Dayton, some to Cincinnati, and some to Monroe. But Detroit was the greatest of them all. It was always a place we wanted to see, but not in the winter of '58. My mother's brother, Andy, was ill, in the hospital, and needing attention.

We rode the "big dog," Greyhound, all day and part of the night to get there. We took a city cab, a real one, for the first time.

The boarding house was ominous, dark, with no appearance of welcome. Uncle Andy also ran a restaurant called the Royal Gardens a couple of blocks over on Bagley, a genuine "greasy spoon" with the best and hottest French fries you ever put in your mouth.

It took only a few minutes to determine that there was no heat and no phone. No one in the other apartments was willing to answer at their door. They were either gone or didn't answer to strangers.

Now what? We searched for a phone. Aunt Kitty lived across town, and all we had to do was call. It was cold, and we walked the streets looking for a phone. The wind was biting, the city stunk, and the snow was deep and made for an uneven stride. It occurred to me that there were few places as desolate as the downtown of a major city. Something there seemed to be un-welcoming, and I could hardly imagine why so many looked upon it as a promised land.

Mom said they might not have enough "bedding," so we all carried blankets and pillows from the boarding house. The items were heavy, but they protected us somewhat from the cold, or at least allowed us to bury one side of our faces in them.

After walking two blocks, we found a gray unlighted filling station. There was barely enough room to stand in the office as the owner reluctantly agreed to allow us use of the phone. In the days of dial phones a small lock secured its use. The owner allowed us to call and wait until Cousin Jim arrived. A quick trip to another row house and we were warm again. I promised myself I would never return until warm weather. I wondered, are there people who live each day looking for shelter?

Detroit Diaspora

A large number of us saw or found our place in the great diaspora of rural people in Appalachia who went after prosperity or at least a better life in metropolitan centers of the north. They called us hillbillies, red-necks, yokels and a number of names we would not repeat in front of the children.

What happened to all the people who left for the promised land in the 1950s and 1960s? How many jobs could you find in Detroit, Dayton, Cincinnati, Toledo, Monroe, and Indianapolis?

James, you and I have been sitting on porches and having reunions all our lives at Turkey Creek, Manchester Street, Andy's bar on Bagley or here at what was the Judge's house. We're still no more than 10 miles from Turkey Creek. If Judge Knuckles were alive he would swear that the barbarians had invaded his home. The sound of the rain on a tin roof and your guitar seems to make it all right to be here.

I watched your father play the guitar when I was a child. I have watched you play since the 1950s. You had a 1951 Ford and worked for Cadillac. Everything in our lives has changed but the music. The first time I saw you play I could swear you had a hundred fingers. It still amazes me.

When we started, I was a child and you were an adult. Now we are men, old men. We have stood at gravesides, buried family, seen our children married, found new homes, and rode the bus to Detroit so many times. Everything has changed and nothing has changed.

Last month we buried your sister, Jewel. We number our days. We shall ask, but we can only answer in music and metaphors. How long will the music play? How many stories can we tell? It's late. We sat here and watched the sun go down, and if we do this a little longer we'll be able to watch it come up.

I'm going to bed. This rocking chair is killing me, and I can hear the music of Bill Monroe.

Turkey Creek and Aunt Kittie

This is how I remember it
now that I am grown.

There is a picture on the wall,
saved years ago from a 1950s family album.

I remember our mother taking us to town

And asking people for a ride to Turkey Creek.

Her sister, Kitty, lived in the house on the hill.

It felt a lot like home.

Two boys, my brother and I,
stood in front of a small board and batten house.

We are four and six years old, dressed in striped
T shirts and short pants.

The wood is unpainted
and the foundations are stacked stones,

found where the highway was cut
through this small mountain.

While I was there:

I saw a dirt road.
It looked like a way out of here.

I heard thunder.
It sounded like God walking.

I felt the air move
from the trucks on the highway.

I tasted watermelon.
It tasted like 1951.

I smelled wood burning.
It smelled like aunt Kitty's stove.

We went down to the highway
hoping to catch a ride back to town.

The new highway
took all but the memories away.

Mexico

They said we were going to Mexico. We had been there before, or at least part of the way. We had come to Turkey Creek before.

Turkey Creek was just a post office-store, a few board and batten houses built by their occupants or a friend and a church house. Aunt Kitty's house was on top of the hill. State highway 25E had been cut through on the way to Barbourville. From her house you could hear the whine of traffic going by.

I was sixteen, my brother fourteen. We had come that day to bury Aunt Kitty's husband, Jim. We rode with the family in the funeral home limousine. We were dressed for the funeral like we were going to church. Everyone had a long coat, gloves, boots, and even the men and boys had hats or caps.

The wind was cold and cutting and the sun was barely above us between the blue mountains of this small southeastern Kentucky community. The hearse moved whisper quiet ahead as we walked behind for a while. The undertaker motioned for us to help move the coffin from the rear of the hearse on to the bed of a wagon. Two mules marched in perfect time to the clicking sounds of its driver. We were walking in a dry creek bed.

I knew the wind would cut me in half. There were barely enough men including me to carry the coffin. Women in long full coats and dresses seemed to drift along the gravel road surface. They told me that we're going up the hill to the grave. We walked in perfect cadence for the first few steps; then we responded to the contour of the hill. I knew we would surely get there, but not soon. There was no snow on the foot path. The ground was frozen and I felt I could not trust my ankles.

Under the poplar trees there was a clearing for this event. It was an ancient cemetery. Some stones were so old they could not be read. Others showed signs of having been only marker stones. Before we could rest the coffin on the straps to be lowered, the chill had already gone to the bone. I shifted from one foot to another to make the shaking stop. The preacher in a rasping and almost desperate unheard voice asked the Lord for enough breath to keep moving.

I thought, "Why in this world did someone name this place Mexico?" Here we were, two miles from Turkey Creek on the way to Stinking Creek. No one had ever met or seen a Mexican as far as I could remember. Maybe Mexico was the most distant place anyone had ever heard about. Country funerals demanded a good bit of time and some music. It was mercifully short today. In a few minutes we were on our way home. I often imagine him lying there, in Mexico.

John Sparks Johnson

The fog lies heavy between the mountains leaving a surreal feeling of being somewhere between dreams and almost awake. The hills of eastern Kentucky are visible during short winter days between ten in the morning and five in the afternoon. The mountains are old and in some places because of the fog they are called "smokies." A ribbon of asphalt vanishes into the fog and then reappears halfway up the mountain near Harlan. It is four o'clock in the morning, and John is on his way back to Sinking Creek from Virginia.

John drives his 1957 International truck made up of pieces from differing models and years. The paint is almost the color of the primer and coal dust. The pitch-black pre-dawn hours are filled with silence interrupted only with the moaning of the motor and strain and twisting noises of the wood and metal of his empty log truck. The brakes sometimes cry and moan. If it were not for the moon, the lights might not be enough.

John is at least fifty years old. The wear and tear on his arms and face tell of years in the mines, saw mills and farm fields. His hands and arms carry the blue tattoos of digging coal. John is not a tall man but his lean silhouette makes him appear so. Most weeks he makes a hundred fifty mile round-trip three or four times to Virginia from Eastern Kentucky to sell a load of timber for use as mine props. What he makes feeds and clothes his wife and two daughters.

Sinking Creek Baptist Church, called "Sinkin" by its members, is a small, pretty, white-board church typical of those in the hills of Kentucky, Virginia, Tennessee, Georgia, and Alabama. Its history is recorded in the cemetery just up the hill.

The music, prayers, and preaching have changed little in these communities since ancestors brought their worship from England, Scotland, Ireland and Wales. The buildings have been built, rebuilt, and remodeled. Teachings include "love thy neighbor, love thy God, live right, and do missions."

Last Sunday morning the men gathered at the side door of the church under the small porch. The topic that morning concerned the Church's note at the bank due the end of the month. Everyone agreed it's a problem.

As John and the preacher are the last to enter the church building, John whispered to the preacher, "I'll have the note money for you on Friday." The preacher knows and John knows that this will simply mean one more day of sawmilling and one more all night haul to Virginia. No one else will ever know the source of the money except the preacher, John, and his wife Etsie.

A License to Drive

She loved teaching with all her heart and preferred one-room schools in distant places no one else would attempt. Being a substitute teacher was wonderfully flexible for a mother of two elementary age boys.

Alice, my mother, began teaching at the age of sixteen. Her first school was a one-room school on Hale's Creek that served as school, community center, and church.

Her mode of transportation in 1925 was a mule named Bob. Not everyone had a car in 1957. If you were going to be a substitute teacher, you had to find some way other than to hitchhike your way to school.

The community was known as Stinking Creek. Laugh not. It was the birthplace of a young lady known as Norma Jean Baker (a.k.a., Marilyn Monroe).

Alice married Bill at thirty-two, had two boys, and returned to teaching when my younger brother entered first grade.

She kept on teaching and going to school. She attended Barbourville Baptist Institute to get her high school diploma and then began taking college courses one at a time while she worked. She went to college every summer and weekends for decades until she had all but one course needed for a degree. To continue teaching, she had to earn the required credits each year to keep her teaching certificate.

The college was across the street from our house. Mom, my brother, and I were all enrolled at the same time. We dared not drop out. If she could work and keep going to college, we had to stay ahead of her.

One day, without warning, she announced that she had bought a Buick from a married college student for $300. It was a "land yacht." But, when you started the motor it was as smooth as a Swiss watch. We painted it in the yard with a brush. The result was a texture not unlike that of an orange.

We desperately wanted whitewall tires and could not figure how we could break down the tires in the yard to apply add-on whitewalls. So we bought some whitewall paint. It was intended to refresh the scuffed white on the side of the tires. We applied multiple coats of this latex. When it rained the paint ran and then dried. If you watched it in motion, the result was somewhat psychedelic.

My father had spent his life in the coal mines and never owned a car. I was thirteen and had been driving my uncle's jeep in cow pastures. By now, Dad owned a grocery store two doors down from the house. I can still hear him shouting at my mother as she drove by the store to town, "Alice, you're going to get them boys killed."

Mom was a good student and passed the written test for driving on the first try. The road test was something else. She may hold the state record for the number of attempts. Every Monday, road tests were given beginning downtown at the courthouse. Mom would go to town, and we would wait hopefully.

I was not the first one home from school that Monday afternoon. My younger brother Sam met me on the porch with the news. When he got home, Mom met him with tears and was hardly able to speak. He replied, "Mom, you've flunked that test before. Now what happened today?" After a couple of attempts and his insistence she was able to say, "I broke the bill off the officer's hat!" Apparently his head had visited the windshield. Silence followed. When Sam told me, I had the taste of copper in my mouth. Why should I be afraid?

Sure enough, with the passage of more Mondays, and perhaps for the fear of his own safety, the officer awarded mom a Kentucky driver's license. We celebrated as if we had won World War III.

In the years ahead, she would teach in places such as Boone Heights, Heidrick, Swan Pond, Trace Branch, Stinking Creek, and finally completing her career at her most beloved, Haven School, at Disappointment, Kentucky. Mom had her license. No offer was ever made to replace the officer's hat.

Last Words

When Sam began Mom's eulogy with the words, "Four hundred years ago . . . " I knew we were in trouble. Lawyers are like that. Everything is presented as to a jury in great detail.

Recounting the industrial revolution, immigration of three classes of people from Scotland, and the history of one-room schools in pioneer America told part of the tale. I did a short tribute, not from caring less, but to manage the temptation to cover a lifetime in a few choice words.

The music included her favorite hymns presented by nephews and nieces. It was Mama's funeral. The house was where Grandma's funeral had been held. It had been a grand home, seven rooms with a front "parlor" or music room. Facing the street was a large bay window from ceiling to floor. The house literally shone through the winter fog.

525 Manchester Street, Barbourville, Kentucky, sat in the Cumberland valley. The house had suffered the floods of the Cumberland River at least three times and been remodeled after the waters receded. Everything imaginable had been replaced, repainted, and repaired. Everything but the floor joists had been refinished and repaired.

Many times as a child I had watched my father put all the furniture up on wooden horses awaiting the impending flood. One February morning he even came to get us boys in a boat, having to break the ice to get close to the house. The sitting room at the front was the perfect place for an at-home funeral.

In Southeastern Kentucky the mountain ridges captured the fog. Some days it did not lift until midmorning, and it settled in again in late afternoon.

On a January day such as this, the cold, damp and shadowed valley added to the solemnity. Mama had lain in state in the house all night, and I was the one who agreed to spend the night with her. I was anxious, weary, and pumped for the day.

The voices were hushed and whispered. Ladies wore subdued colors, and the men were dressed as if it were Sunday. The laughter, singing and playing of the children had a different tone than at other family gatherings.

In a town of less than 3000, everybody knows everybody's business. The local dignitaries were there, the bank president, chairman of the school board, doctors, lawyers, teachers, and professors. Alice had taught most of them and their parents. There must have been 30 people in a house that had not seen that many in decades.

A "Do it Your Self Funeral" was what we wanted and decided was appropriate, knowing Mama's attitude about such. We had rarely been chastised for being bashful. It echoed what Americans had done for decades before such events were subcontracted to clergy.

Built in the 1880s, this house was no stranger to a funeral in the parlor for a family member. Nan, our paternal grandmother, had celebrated her "homegoing" in this very parlor in the 1950s.

A good funeral is a once in a lifetime affair. You had to know Mama to have understood this. Alice always had the last word. She was the original "I'll do it my way" woman. Forty years of teaching one-room schools, riding a mule to work, and being married to a coal miner had made her tough. She had been the caregiver in her family. Brothers and sisters came to her house to be cared for before dying. She did hospice before it was included on any insurance form. The question was, "What would Mama do if she were here?" Whatever it was, it would be done her way.

Uncle Dave's two adult children, David and Margaret, sang an old Welsh hymn in perfect pitch and harmony. Mama wouldn't have given you a dime for some of the songs, except when these two sang. She had requested such traditional pieces as "Jerusalem" and "Amazing Grace." At least one "high church" hymn such as "O God Our Help In Ages Past" seemed to suit them well, as they stood postured in their Sunday best.

Then it happened. Thunder under the parlor floor. No one said a word. The musicians did not miss a beat. Every pair of eyes in the room rotated in search of the offending noise. This group was unarmed, at least for the funeral. Surely no one would "cherry bomb" Mama's funeral. I know she had occasionally offended a public figure, but ... .

The second verse offered perfect timing and pitch plus the sound of a piercing crack followed by two more volleys from below. The floor began to fall, not far, just a couple of inches. "The floor joists have failed," announced Sam. He is the family member assigned to deal with any crisis.

Our son-in-law, Clift, reared in the funeral home business, and sitting conveniently close to the coffin, was calculating which way Mama's coffin would tilt. He's a fine young man, with great poise, a very professional appearance, and considerably less than 150 pounds. He looked somewhat at risk on the low side of the casket. The best I could do would be to fling myself on the floor and soften the fall.

Half the people, including the musicians, fled to the dining room. Some headed for the front door. The children laughed, screamed, and cried.

Brother Sam admonished us again to stay where we were; the floor in the dining room might be less secure. More out of fear than anything else, the group was frozen. It was too late not to continue the service. The house would either fall or not fall. We were in this thing together. We'd manage. At least at the graveside we'd be standing on terra firma.

Alice, you did it again. Yours is the last word.

Another Bill

I knew him from a small-town church. Bill's father was a country physician in small-town Appalachia. They always encouraged boys and girls to get an education.

Whenever we participated in "youth week" at church, were honored for anything in the community or school, or graduated from high school, there was always an acknowledgement from Bill, even long after his father had died. I have no idea how many students he encouraged over the years.

Bill graduated from seminary in Church Music, had voice problems, and then entered the business community. He was a success. As far back as I can remember, he had a new Cadillac and a new Corvette. For a small town in the fifties and sixties, this seemed exceptional. Any time the high school or church had a fund-raising carwash, I could count on him. Not only that, I got to pick the cars up and bring them back.

Bill was an avid fan of the Indianapolis 500. In the 1960s he would order films of the race and invite everyone interested to come by the office for a viewing. That tiny office was filled with men watching the race and shouting like we were in the stands. For a teenager, to be included was exciting.

Bill never married. He took care of his mother and father until they died. He took care of his aunt who lived next door until she died, and a girlfriend who lived with him until she died.

I do not remember who told me first. At the time he would have been in his forties. Someone entered his home and murdered Bill. They emptied a pistol into his body, tore out the phone, and left. Whatever investigation followed produced nothing.

Now fifty years later I continue to be curious. Friends who still live there now tell me no one was ever caught. It leaves a profound sense of incompleteness. Perhaps it rarely ever crosses anyone's mind now. I wonder if the murderer is still alive and what he thinks. I wonder who goes unblessed because of Bill's absence.

Church Tales

Baptizing at the Brickyard

I can remember living in a small town across the street from white frame homes, stone houses, a trailer park, a college and a couple of blocks from the Brickyard Ponds. I remember well going through the Brickyard and looking into the gas-fired kilns as the bricks were made.

Bricks required clay. The digging of clay left large holes that filled with water. Someone did the community a favor and stocked the water holes with fish, thus the Brickyard Ponds. In a small town they provided a good bit of entertainment: fishing, boating, swimming, frog gigging, etc.

They also attracted a number of people who perhaps had too much to drink. They gathered to swim, swing out on grape vines and dive into the deep end. They brought friends for a romantic gathering place during the evenings.

Holidays and Sundays sometimes would allow for a gathering for church groups and a baptizing for congregations that had neither a building nor a baptistry. Remember here that the ecclesiology of many Baptist, Pentecostal, Holiness, and other congregations required baptism by immersion. It was deep enough. It was close enough for the neighbors to hear the singing and shouting and attract a crowd of the curious.

Candidates for baptism were often serious and celebratory. Ladies in white dresses came out of the waters dripping with a slight tint of tan from the clay. Children ran out and dogs barked and chased the children.

"Uncle Grant," as he was known, was a local gentleman aspiring to do better. He presented himself for re-baptism most years and was re-baptized in the pond.

One summer he approached the water, stuck his right foot in and promptly exclaimed, "Whoo—Preacher, this water is colder than Hell!" The Preacher had expected as much and immediately immersed him. Deacons led him to a place behind sheets strung on wire that served as a dressing room.

A few summers later Uncle Grant returned to be re-baptized. Apparently, the earlier attempt had not had the desired effect. He was ceremoniously led into the water, immersed and raised up. It was August and oppressively hot. He raised his hand in a manner to suggest that he wanted to say something appropriate. The only words he could manage were "A Merry Christmas to you all!" We could not decide if he was six months early or six months late.

Funeral: It's Not What You Thought

It was a lovely day for a funeral. We were in the process of remodeling the Scrap Iron Chapel, a name borrowed from a group of older men who met there for Bible Study. It was a typical gothic building with a lot of blond wood and a bright green carpet.

The ladies of the church decided that it deserved better. The pews were sent out for refinishing and the carpet was to be replaced. Tommy, the carpet installer, and his men were ready to go. They were a most efficient group, who were at least fashion challenged for a funeral. No funeral was on the schedule. They knelt on the floor with their hawk-billed knives ready to cut spaces for inserting the pew anchors.

It occurred to me that this was good, but perhaps we should see if a coffin could be brought down the aisle before determining the final placement of pews. I called the funeral home and inquired if they might lend a casket for this test. They were agreeable and sent one posthaste.

The casket arrived in a hearse with a driver. It was immediately apparent that we would have to do the lifting. Three installers, a hearse driver, and I hoisted the casket on to the carriage and wheeled it up the steps and into the chapel. We rolled it down the aisle, centered it in front of the pulpit, invited the minister of worship to come and inspect it for his purposes and then rolled it out, placed it in the hearse and bid the driver farewell.

Good church members and particularly deacons guide us often in the proper way to do our work. Deacon Frazier, a Court Reporter whose office window looked out upon the front door of the Chapel, was instantly present. I have known few people who have cared as much for the "least of these" as Cary.

"What have you done? This person deserves more respect than that! I've never seen a funeral take less than ten minutes!"

I responded, "Cary, don't believe your lying eyes! This was only a test." This was a funeral that did not happen.

Leonard Filardo

It has been almost fifty years and I owe a "thank you" to Leonard Filardo. He came to our church as many do with their families. I knew very little except that he was perhaps a first generation Italian immigrant who had found a loving family in Nashville and joined a welcoming church congregation. He was at least sixty years old, tanned from a lifetime outside as a day laborer.

I doubt that he will even be mentioned in the Church history. We had completed most of the construction on a new sanctuary. He had watched the construction process with great curiosity. His suggestions were useful and intelligent.

Leonard would not stand and speak to a group. He would not serve on a committee and had limited financial resources. He asked if I would go with him to a large unfinished space beneath the worship area. There was little or no money left for another project.

The area was at least thirty feet wide and sixty feet long. There were foundation walls at least eight feet high. The only problem was that no one had planned to use the space. He would dig it out and make it useful if we would pour a floor. Leonard said that he would like permission to bring a wheelbarrow, his shovels and pick axes and rent a jack hammer. What did we have to lose?

He came every morning at eight and worked most days. I tried to help him when I could. Others tried also but we all found it too demanding. Leonard kept on working. In a few months we celebrated the pouring of a floor and the use of the space. I remember the look on his face. No one had to tell him this was a worthy task and a great gift to the congregation.

Leonard taught me that not only this was a worthy task but also a reason for Christ coming as a carpenter.

Misunderstood

It's easy to be misunderstood, particularly if you are a young minister in a Baptist Church, and you believe you can save the world one alcoholic at a time.

I met Art and Betty at church. He was a middle-aged man who made his living selling carpet. He had done quite well, enjoyed the good life, owned a typical three- bedroom home, and a new Plymouth. Periodically Betty would fall victim to too much drink and then call me to tell me Art was drunk.

I responded with a call to missions and to rescue Art. She somehow managed to live on the border of drunk. I told her I would do what I could. She knew I would understand. He consented to being rescued. I separated him from the alcohol in the house and went home for the evening.

The next evening I checked on him and found him drunk again, removed his current supply of alcohol, and stayed for a while until he fell asleep. I thought we were making progress. About two o'clock in morning Betty called and tells me he's drunk again.

I got in my car and drove the mile or so to their home. Art was sitting in his chair with a bottle in his hand. I'm tired and exhausted. We had a few words. "Are you ready for detox?" was the question. Apparently he was, or at least he sought to quiet me. I needed to get the bottle away from him and get him in the car.

We struggled with the bottle. Yes, he wanted to go, but letting go of the bottle was a separate issue. He had been up for days, he was weak and let go of the bottle. In the process he spilled it all over me. I had not shaved, my hair was a mess and my clothes were disheveled. Calls every hour of the night from Art and Betty had been exhaustive. Art demanded that we take his new Plymouth if we were going to detox.

We drove through downtown. It was two thirty a.m. What would I tell the police if they pull me over?

"Yes, Sir, I understand. I'm Art's clergyman and we are on the way to detox! No, I've had nothing to drink. I'm sorry I smell bad and my eyes are bloodshot. No, this is not my car and I don't have registration and insurance for it." Well, at least we made it to the hospital without being stopped. I'm sure the police would understand.

With the assistance of a waiting orderly, we got Art into a wheelchair and waited for a nurse to see us. I explained that I was Art's minister to the nice lady at the emergency room desk. I could tell by the way she looked at me, she understood.

We waited patiently, and finally were wheeled into one of the emergency rooms. I declared, "I'm here to get Art into detox." That was obvious. The nurse began the process of interview with the standard form. Art sort of chuckled as she asks each question. Some questions had to be repeated. I worked enough nights as a night orderly in a small hospital to realize how one operates in a semi-sleep state. Filling out forms is one of the most boring of tasks.

Sometimes one forgets and just goes to the next question whether it applies to this patient or not. Sometimes a question might be misunderstood or perhaps understood too well. The nurse asked about some "female" surgery he might have had. This was entertaining for Art and he began to describe his experience with his "female" surgery. He was both understood and misunderstood at the same time.

My understanding of this event is not yet complete. It is one of those events that you would gladly have missed but find at least curious. Understand?

Hope for Healing

Broad Street in Rome on Sunday evenings is peaceful. Broad Street is four lanes wide with little traffic for a "revival" meeting dismissing at the City Auditorium. "Revival" is a religious southern tradition often following the harvest of summer crops. This one was advertised as of significant import considering the preacher was one Televangelist Ernest Angley. Much had been expected. The sign outside stated that there would be healings tonight and all week.

The meeting had ceased. Most everyone had left except those clearing the building, loading equipment, or disscussing theology with the evangelist.

It had rained most of the day, with intermittent reprieve as the crowd moved in and out. A lone Ford F150 long bed pickup truck was next to the curb at the foot of the steps. The truck showed some wear. One fender was obviously a replacement. Its primer coat did not match the two-toned red and cream color of the rest of the vehicle.

The bed of the truck was framed in pipe. Across the top of the frame was a tarp, hopefully to protect the cargo or those who rode in the rear from some of the rain. The motor was idling, the tailgate was

58

down, and two 2 by 12s served as a wheelchair ramp. A metal lawn chair faced backward on the passenger side of the truck bed.

Two large young men in starched "Big Ben" Overalls and white shirts escorted a wheelchair with "Mama" in it down the handicap ramp and up their ramp into the back of the truck. The men had the appearance of day laborers who could lift. At the tailgate they pushed "Mama's" wheelchair with her in it carefully into the bed of the truck. One of the sons rotated the wheelchair and backed it up to the rear window. The other son tied the chair to the pipe frame that held the tarp and took his place in the metal lawn chair next to Mama.

The tailgate was latched, the ramp boards pushed into the bed, and a red "flag" attached to the end of one board.

The son who would drive entered the cab. Quietly and with much care the truck made a "U" turn in the street and slowly moved out of sight.

Apparently, healing had not taken place. Jesus had been there the whole time.

We Don't Know You!

I have searched my memory, but the name of the church is no longer there. Newly married, full of ambition, I had decided to enter the social work school at seminary. That was great but it required 12 hours a week of field work, unpaid. The job on the grounds crew was not enough.

Fortunately, I met the Director of the Kentucky Temperance League at church and was offered the lucrative opportunity of travelling with his group each Sunday to distant churches across the state to carry the message of the evils of drink. For this I would receive $25 honoraria, out of which I had to pay for one or maybe two meals.

Most of the time it was an easy task: Meet the team at 5:00 a.m. Ride for three or four hours. Get out at a church and do a Bible Study at 9:45 a.m. and ask them to transport me to the next church for Sunday morning worship. Wait on the church steps to be picked up around 3:00 p.m. How difficult could it be?

We came to a screeching halt at the front door of a red brick church like thousands of churches across the nation. They left and I went in to find a couple of aging Sunday School Secretaries. "Hi, I'm Bill Davies with the Temperance League." No more needed be said. Apparently, they had anticipated my arrival and responded with a monotone, "We don't know you and we didn't send for you." I knew nothing would happen here. I asked if someone would give me a ride to the next church. The response was repeated, "We don't know you and we didn't send for you." I left.

Standing on the street outside, I tried to figure my options. Having been raised in a small town, I knew the police to be willing to help a stranger in town. In a few minutes I was able to flag down a Sheriff's car. His response was to take me to a taxi driver. I had a $20 in my pocket. It was enough to get a ride to my next small town.

I sat, waited, and almost burst into tears at the sight of my ride home. Somewhere, come Judgment Day, there will be some justice. I wonder if, when those two Sunday School Secretaries approach the Pearly Gates, the answer to their inquiry will be, "We don't know you and we didn't send for you."

Hunger and Homelessness

Abandoned

We gathered, as we had each Tuesday since 2003, at First Methodist Church for Meals and More, extending a caring hand and a bag meal for anyone who is hungry.

Most of our guests are street people with a variety of needs. Some are homeless and living outside in cars, on decks, in abandoned buildings, under bridges, in the shrubs, or sofa surfing at a friend's home.

A slow, cold, constant rain had been going all day with a high temperature in the 40s. Rome was under a flood warning.

In spite of the constant rain, approximately thirty some hungry souls gathered in the meeting room anticipating a bag meal.

One gentleman presented himself for a meal and asked if we knew of somewhere he might find shelter. He was probably fifty years old, black, and wearing two or three layers of clothes with a hood. His speech was diminutive, and he returned to the question, "Do you know of somewhere I can stay?"

My question was, "What is your name and where did you spend last night?"

"My name is John, and I slept outside under a bridge."

He returned to a chair in a distant corner of the room and pulled his hood up over his head.

I called the Davies Shelter and Salvation Army. Both were full. We agreed we would call back around 6:00 p.m.

The crowd had gathered. We waited until 5:20 p.m. to pass out seconds from the remaining inventory of meals. Those waiting took extra meals, and the table was emptied. The rain intensified, and still no beds were available.

As we discussed the crisis for John, one of our gentlemen guests overheard and said, "He can stay with me." I knew Eugene. He and his wife had been living in abandoned structures for at least a year.

Horace, co-leader of Meals and More, Mac, our grandson who was volunteering for the evening, John, Eugene, and I loaded in my Jeep and headed south in the wind and rain. As we approached one house, Eugene said, "Pull over here." I recognized it as an abandoned house among other abandoned houses. John and Eugene jumped out and waved us on in the moving traffic past a police car.

It occurred that I had been party to their accommodations. Now we have an abandoned house and, more tragically, two abandoned men.

A Meal on the Way to Hell

My wife and I sat down for a quiet dinner in a local diner. It was a Barbeque place, one of those that make the South what it is.

It was unbearably hot and you could see people moving through the parking lot and down the avenue leaving town. I noticed a familiar face looking through the massive windows, deciding whether he would enter or not. He was figuring the odds.

He was a short, skinny, disheveled-looking man of approximately 60 years. I had known him from soup kitchens and food lines around town for years. He was consistent. Every time I saw him, he made an appeal for a small amount of money for a meal, personal items, cigarettes, or bus fare.

The money for any of the aforementioned items could also provide money for alcohol. He knew I would not believe him, but he felt it was always worth a try.

He walked the ten steps into the restaurant, smiled, greeted me, and immediately let me know he sure would like a hamburger. The waitress, whom I could see, and apparently the owner, whom I could not see, had known him.

I told the waitress, "Get him a hamburger and a drink and put it on my bill." I had no more spoken than the owner escorted him out with great efficiency. All of us saw the futility of his trying to get a free meal.

We continued and enjoyed our meal. Out of the corner of my eye I watched our friend cross in front of the restaurant and go just out of sight. I knew he would be there on our exit.

We paid our bill and started out into the parking lot. The manager approached with the declaration, "That man out there is going to hell!"

Outside, I told our friend to come and see me at the food pantry and I would get him something to eat. I don't know what the owner's recommended destination for me was.

Archie

Archie—toothless, bald, and bearded—roams the streets he calls home. I have rarely seen him without a group of friends. One of his friends handed me Archie's I.D. when I asked who he was. Somehow these guys have so few attachments that they easily share identities. Maybe this is the opposite of an "identity crisis."

Most of my understanding of Archie does not come from Archie, but from his friends. Archie is a dental professional's challenge. Every tooth in his head is missing. His gums flap with each verbal response. Someone failed to tell Archie that when you have no teeth you must slow down to enunciate. Archie's communications are troubling. It takes one a while to learn some of his words and to be able to fill in the remainder of any story or pleading.

A number of local "do-gooders" have worked hard to raise Archie's status in life. They have managed to help him have some disability income and housing. He knows well where every soup kitchen meets for each week of the month.

However, Archie prefers not to live within the constriction of provided housing. Just the presence of someone else, such as a neighbor, a visitor, or a bureaucrat, seems to be more supervision than he is willing to accept.

I have not seen him in a while—Archie, make yourself known.

Asher

Jacob wrestled all night with the angel until the angel blessed him. He would not let go of the angel until he got his blessing. Jacob had a son. He named him Asher. In Hebrew the name Asher means blessing. I have seen it every day at the homeless shelter. Some wrestle with demons and some wrestle with angels.

Asher was a young man who had the appearance of being ten years older. He was straight out of the lyrics of the Willie Nelson song *Poncho and Lefty*: "Now you wear your skin like iron, your breath as hard as kerosene." Yet underneath it all, he had a winning smile and gracious heart.

He had obeyed all the rules, helped keep the homeless shelter clean, found a job, and saved everything he made in order to pay his deposit on an apartment in a shotgun house downtown. It was a perfect example of what a slumlord would offer. It was modestly furnished with holes in both the ceiling and floor.

Allison, Shelter Director, and I loaded both our vehicles and helped him move in. It was at least dry and warm. I knew the neighborhood. Rumors and sightings of drugs, whores, and drunks were not hard to believe. At least he was close enough to walk to his job.

Asher had been in my Sunday evening Bible study for the months he had been at the Shelter. After eleven years of teaching on Sundays, I occasionally get a hint that someone has been listening. I told them the story I heard Lofton Hudson teach five decades ago in seminary. It would become a book and the theme of my ministry. The thesis is that God has blessed us and has granted us the power to bless others. The blessings God has given us mean nothing if they are not used to bless the lives of others.

As we turned to leave after moving him in, Asher said, "Can I ask one favor?" Why not? We have come this far.

"Would you bless my house?" It took my breath away. Allison was similarly taken aback.

We three stopped and held hands. I prayed for God's peace and presence to be in this place and in Asher's life. I prayed that he might be blessed in order to bless others. I prayed that God would protect him from the evil one. And then I prayed a prayer of thanksgiving to God for bringing Asher into our lives. Asher means blessing. Amen.

Worth Saving

Nothing has changed for the two story, stucco building just across the bridge one block from downtown. You could pass it for years and not even know it was there. They told me it was the Star House, where we would be doing a Bible study. The Star House is a recovery shelter for alcoholic men and women.

Harold and I had volunteered to do the Bible Study for the men's division. Harold was a World War II veteran and one of those who were on the beach at Normandy. Always the Bible stories were presented so the men could share their own experiences. Their stories were varied and many times startling. We learned to laugh a lot and cry a little. We were four or five years into the effort.

It has changed little over thirty years. As you enter there is a small office to the right, a family-like living room, a small room with books and a table, furnished with obviously used and rescued furniture and books. Across the back of the building is the small kitchen and dining room. The walls are off white, stained with years of tobacco smoke. There is a small table and vinyl covered chairs. A thousand stories have been told here over meals and afterward.

On this Sunday evening, the man across from me was fifty plus and by no means a small man, over six feet tall, heavy with a soft cultured voice. He politely identified himself as Donnie and asked if he could speak with us for a few minutes after the Bible Study. He was not as well kept as he might have once been. It showed in his posture, haircut, and eyes. He chain-smoked and his fingers were stained with tobacco.

At the end of the meeting we three remained around the small table. The others had scattered. Donnie renewed his cup of coffee and quietly pushed a piece of paper toward each of us. Before I could turn it over and review it he simply asked, "Do you think I'm worth saving?" To hear any man ask such a question is humbling.

The paper was a statement of net worth: $75. "My name is Donnie. I landed here after being in most of the drunk tanks in north Georgia and sleeping under the bridge. Could I come to the church and talk with you tomorrow?"

Monday morning he appeared at my office declaring, "I've got to get some work!"

"What can you do? What have you done in the past?"

"Well, my resume says I have been a Federal Bank Examiner, but I can't go back there for a while or ever." His well-done resume told that and more. He had two graduate degrees, twenty years of experience, and now was living at an alcohol recovery house.

The shelter was one block from a bank he had examined. "I used to walk in there and tell the Bank President how he should run his business. I can't face them now. I can't walk past that building."

"Donnie, let me make some calls. Maybe I can find some kind of work," I said.

"Okay, just one more favor. I need to go by my house in Euharlee and pick up some clothes. All I have is what I have on my back and what I can find in the clothes closet downstairs."

"Sure. I can go tomorrow" I said. He lived about forty miles from Rome. It should be a pleasant ride.

The next afternoon I pulled up in front of the Star House. He was in the foyer looking out the window and ready to go. This was just another mission of mercy.

We pulled up in front of a dignified, well kept, white frame house. There were plants on the porch and curtains in the windows. I parked the van on the wrong side of the street directly in front of the house. Donnie came around behind me and opened the driver's side rear door. I thought it was for his convenience in loading his clothes. He did not invite me inside. Five minutes later he was leaping off the front porch, running and shouting at the top of his voice as he dove into the back seat. "Drive. Get the hell out of here."

I did just that. I had no idea his ex-wife had a restraining order. He chose not to tell me. I didn't know he was "breaking and entering," and I didn't know what was happening, but it appeared to me that there was no advantage in staying. Was his wife there and was she armed? He said no when I inquired. I had no intention of driving a "get away" car. What's the statute of limitations on stupidity?

It was a long trip back to the Star House with explanations and apologies. Within weeks I found him a job at a car wash.

For weeks I would see him. He always thanked me for finding him the car washing job. It was February, and on some days his clothes would freeze. Six months later he said, "I found a bank that will give me a job as a teller."

"Go for it." I said. Without fanfare, he moved from Rome.

For months every week on Friday evenings, Harold or I would get a call. "Still got my job." Then, "Hey, guess what? I'm a loan officer." For years he called. "I'm VP now. Guess What? These fools offered me a job as bank president." He told me his daughter had come to live with him while she completed her college. Later he founded two loan companies. I hoped he would come back to visit, but he never did.

The calls continued. I heard from Harold that Donnie had what he called the "Big C," cancer. Occasionally there was a call and then nothing. I heard he was "gone." I pass the Star House almost every day. Rarely do I go by without thinking of him. There may be one resident that remembers Donnie. I can say his name to Harold and he never fails to smile. Harold is now in his nineties.

"Breaking and entering?" How much time do you get for aiding and abetting in the theft of someone's own laundry?

Feet Hurt

Feet hurt? I watched him walk through the soup line.
    It wasn't the first time.

He looked like all the others,
    dispossessed sisters and brothers.

Feet hurt? Shoes, he said he needed some.
    He knew not from whence they would come.

I knew another man, one of a kind.
    He was a loner, building an empire in his time.

How are the hungry, how are the homeless?
    Are they finding a place to rest?

Feet Hurt? They walk the streets of Rome
    like the Israelites looking for home.

They walk now in borrowed shoes.
    Blessed by someone who paid his dues.

Luke

It's happened again. Some bureaucrat in a mental health facility decided that at least one of his clients needed to be dismissed. He took up too much space and used too many resources. His caseworker said he didn't know what to do, so he loaded him up with two more patients and told the night orderly to deliver these three to the Salvation Army and the Davies Shelter in Rome, Georgia.

The driver was ordered not to call ahead. Just load them up. "Deliver them to the two addresses in Rome. Get them out of the car and drive away. Do not ask if they can stay."

The temperature was forty-four degrees and raining.

Luke was in his mid-thirties. His hair was blond and his eyes were piercing blue. His skinny frame stood at the front door on South Broad. He was soaking wet, wore khakis, a tee shirt, no socks, no shoes, and no medication, just like he was when ordered to get in the van. When he asked about his destination he was simply told, "A better place."

Luke was chilled to the bone. His teeth were chattering. His breath came in short, shallow breaths, and he found himself stuttering because of the cold.

When confronted, Luke's prior caregivers had to admit their error and sent a cab to get him. They told us they were not aware that he had no socks when he left. Maybe we won in confronting them. But did Luke win? We didn't have the psychiatric resources to care for him. Who knows where he is today?

Luke means light. Is he living in the light or barely on the edge? The apostle John speaks of a battle between the dark and the light. Maybe Luke is a casualty of this battle.

Ichabod

I saw him as I drove down South Broad. I rarely offered a ride but could not resist.

He looked like he always did, but a little more ragged. Ichabod was thirty years old, with the face of a fifteen-year old. He was a child who had been on his own -or years. He had discovered alcohol and drugs.

"How've you been?" I asked. We both knew he had been struggling. He had the appearance and smell of living outside. It was rough now, January. If he could make it outside a few more weeks he would be able to survive outside.

Ick hadn't shaved for a few days. His hands showed the wear of being an apprentice and a licensed plumber for some years. He always had work but not always a driver's license. The money was good as long as family, friends, and those with drugs and issues were absent. Returns home only added to his problems.

Ichabod is the Old Testament word meaning, "the glory of the Lord has forsaken thee." I remember when he lived with us at the shelter. He was always the first to say, "Thank you." Any time I saw him he would tell me, "Buy the parts and I'll fix anything that's broke." He had done just that. He came to the food pantry and fixed everything in the place. The joy of life and the glory of the Lord was present in this man/child, and yet, you could sense he was weary of the struggle.

This time something was absent. The light in his eyes was dimmed. The smile was offered but it spoke of good things past, not of what was to come. I let him out where he asked downtown. He did not tell me where he was going. I could not bring myself to ask. He was going to sleep in a deserted house, car, or back porch. As he smiled and turned to leave all I could think was Ichabod, "the glory of the Lord has forsaken thee."

Kilion: Help Me Get a Job

Every Tuesday evening for over eleven years, a number of churches in our community came together to provide meals for hungry people, many of whom were on the way home from work. Most of the time it was two or three meals. It's called Meals and More. The emphasis was on "More."

We listened to health concerns, financial difficulties, spiritual challenges, and sometimes the need for employment. Kilion said he needed work. He was stranded in Rome after finding his way down here from up north. He had come to live with family and they had deserted him.

I was a minister at a local church with responsibilities for the care and appearance of the facilities. Each week Kilion begged for work. I didn't have anything. He described his merits. "I work hard. Just ask anyone. I can give references. I have been a painter. I can fix things. I can clean windows."

The last item caught my interest. We had windows. We had windows four floors up. I asked him, "Do you have contractor's insurance?"

"Insurance? Man, I don't have a place to sleep!"

Then I asked, "Why did you leave your last job cleaning windows?"

Calmly and without reservation he responded, "I have fainting spells." I understand that the name Kilion in Hebrew means, "fall and die."

Lazarus

He wore his hat like Charlie Daniels and looked about the size of Willie Nelson. He rarely spoke but never seemed to be without an answer when asked. We called him Rick. He appeared regularly at the basement of the little stone church building on Tuesday evenings in search of a couple of free take-home meals. He always needed shoes. He mostly wore boots, the kind with the pointed toes. He said he could kill a roach in a corner with the toes of his boots. He believed in layers of clothes. Even with two or three layers he was a small man.

I asked him if he had a place to stay. He said, "I'm okay." I pursued the question and suggested that we had room at the shelter. "You know I don't stay inside. I just can't live around people." I remembered having given him a tarp to hang so he could live under the Second Avenue bridge.

For over four years Rick came faithfully to Meals and More. Then he just stopped. In a few weeks we were bothered by his absence. Then we became disturbed. Charlie said he was gone. Alfred said he thought he was dead.

Over the next three weeks, the answer came that Rick had received some kind of government check for a sizable sum and had been murdered for it. Was he lying dead under the bridge? Had they pushed his body into the Oostanoola River? Some said yes. Others simply did not know. Then everything went silent.

Sometimes I would look up and down the river's edge hoping to see him sitting there. Mostly we waited.

Then, like Lazarus, he had the nerve to show up on a Tuesday evening. Someone said, "Damn it, Rick, you're supposed to be dead, murdered for your government money!!!"

"Sorry, I've been all over town."

Aggravated and filled with joy at the same time, I was reminded at how the friends and family of Lazarus must have felt. The best Hebrew translation of Lazarus is, "God's help for a needy beggar."

Porch Guest

I watched a pastor apologize
for something done unwise.

Someone was troubled by the homeless
sleeping on the church porch in distress.

So what do we do about this?
The community and members hiss.

It's an outrage. We cannot allow.
Take care of it and do it now.

Always there is someone bright
To help us do what is right.

It's clean and quiet,
There'll be no public riot...

We'll install sprinkler heads
and soak their makeshift beds.

Think about it.
They voted and did it.

It was efficient,
The body was in agreement.

Walking in the Fog

I can see him walking in the early morning fog north on the Second Avenue bridge. The cool summer morning fog finds its way down town and envelopes what few men and vehicles are out just before daybreak. For eons two rivers have converged here creating a third. There have been people here—hunters, gatherers, settlers, businessmen, traffic, and a few homeless souls. In a small downtown such as this it's not uncommon to see people walking across the bridge.

I first noticed him at Meals and More. He and fifty or so others gather each Tuesday evening for a free take-home meal shared out of the basement of First Christian Church. The church meets in a pre-civil war, white stone building, the stone brought here on wagons, stone by stone, quarried in Elijay, Georgia. For an hour prior to meals, men, women and children gather on the sidewalk to get a place in line. I thought it was to get food. It's more about community than meals.

When the doors opened, Albert Sheppard stood in one of two lines to get one meal and to wait for another if they were not all taken. Tall, lean, a middle-aged black man, he carried himself with more dignity than others in the group. He stood erect. When we shared greetings, it was apparent he had some education and enjoyed his ability to speak. He took pleasure in how he used words.

We got to know each other, shared pleasantries and occasionally a good laugh. He was about my age, sixty plus. I learned he had spent some time in Vietnam. After a few months I could thank him for his service without causing him to retreat.

Yes, he had been in Vietnam and had been trying to qualify for agent-orange benefits for years. No luck. In the months that followed, I promised to see what I might be able to do. I know nothing of the bureaucracy of the Veteran's Administration. It took only a few calls to know he was probably not going to get any help soon, but we kept trying.

In the years ahead, he found his way to the Food Pantry. Cathy, the food pantry coordinator, told me she was the first to interview him. He told her he was "six feet six inches tall and sixty-six years old." The interview took only a few minutes. His photo ID was copied, information was taken, and he was given a bag of some meat and vegetables. In the following months, he returned occasionally.

In the years ahead, he had need of the Shelter. I remember his face in the Sunday Evening Bible Study. He completed his stay at the Shelter in a couple of months and found a cheap second story apartment downtown.

Somewhere we got separated. For a few weeks, then months, his face was not there. No one at the Shelter seemed to know where he went. We knew his next address, but no one there knew anything. Each Tuesday evening at Meals and More, I asked those I thought might know, "Have you seen Albert?" No one knew. Always the answer was the same at the Shelter, the food pantry, and at Meals and More.

It's frustrating to think you could not find someone. The jail knew nothing. Local police did not know. Some at the Tuesday meal told me they thought he was dead. I asked how and where, and they did not know. Some days I asked and some I did not. This search became obsessive on my part. Google search by name and reviewing newspaper records showed nothing.

The Coroner's Office did not know. In frustration I asked to speak to Coroner, Barry Henderson.

He did not know. I told him I thought Albert was a veteran. Did that matter? A second recounting of Albert's description, and he knew Albert. He had Albert's body. We learned Albert was a 16-year veteran of military service with a long tour in Vietnam. He had also been a policeman in Atlanta.

The Veteran's Administration would provide a full military burial. Someone had to claim the body. There was no family to be found. Barry told me someone needed to claim the body, and all I had to do was have a notice posted at the courthouse for forty-eight hours.

How did one come to this place in life or death? Claim a body? Were there any among us valued so little that their remains would be unclaimed? Barry told me how to proceed, and I posted the notice at the courthouse.

Information came around in the days ahead. Someone had a disagreement with Albert, poured something flammable on him, struck a match, and watched him jump out a second story window.

Albert spent some weeks in the burn center in Augusta before dying.

Albert qualified for a full military burial at the National Military Cemetery in Canton, Georgia. Barry made all the arrangements. Atop the mountain it is one of the most beautiful, well kept, park-like sites I have ever seen. Among the hundreds of sites there are a number of covered areas for memorial services.

We gathered under the marble shelter provided for occasions such as this. We had a full military contingent, funeral home personnel, and three adults who came to pay their respects. One was a lady who had met and helped Albert in Rome occasionally when he needed transportation, and there was a couple who came to pay their respects to a veteran.

I read scripture, made comments, prayed, and the flag was presented to one of the ladies who cared enough to attend. Shots from the military gun salute still ring in my ears.

Some were troubled that Albert's passing had not been recognized with a proper memorial service in Rome. Horace Stewart, Co-Pastor of First Christian Church, and co-host of Meals and More offered the hospitality and sanctuary of his church's place of worship.

We passed the word at the next Tuesday's Meals and More that there would be a local memorial service honoring Albert Shepperd, Jr., on the next Tuesday evening following the distribution of meals. Frank Murphy agreed to sing, Beverly

Harris agreed to play the piano, and Horace and I prepared short messages. The Meals and More group has prayed together almost every week, we have shared joy and grief occasionally. Then we came to say good-bye to one of our family.

We gathered in the sanctuary. It was an exceptional group: homeless, clergy, educators, business people, volunteers who serve the hungry and homeless, Bobby, Tony, Carol, L.J. and Serpentfoot. We prayed, sang, read from the Bible, and preached. Albert was dispatched to his eternal reward with all the dignity of veteran and citizen of our community.

Albert, I still see you walking in the fog.

Steve

I can tell you exactly where Steve and I first met. It was one of those meetings where everybody introduced themselves as "Hi, I'm ___, and I'm an alcoholic." We met in a Bible Study at the STAR House, a residential home for recovering alcoholics. Harold and I had already seen a hundred other "Steves" pass through in the prior dozen years.

He was a long, tall, skinny dude of thirty, who looked twenty years beyond his chronology. He had that alcohol induced boniness that caused his knees, elbows, and wrists to almost pierce his skin as they moved loosely when he stood. Taller than average, he walked with that whipped dog, stooped shouldered rhythm that was meant to carry him unnoticed in and out of the room.

When he spoke, you had to lean toward him to decide what he was trying to say. He whispered, "You got any work? I can fix or build anything." And he could. His fingers, stained with years of nicotine, moved like a surgeon. The economy of his motions was a work of art. He hung the fan that turns above my head now. It has born quiet testimony to his skills.

We had long talks about who he was and how he came to be. It took a couple of years to get most of the information. His biography dribbled out in bits and pieces. Some of it came when he was searching for a dry place to sleep. Once or twice the church put him up in a cheap motel. He would do some repairs for the church and save us a few bucks.

With a recommendation he would get a repair job here and there, fixing a light or stove for a widow.

Drunk or sober, I always knew I could trust Steve. Some guys were too lazy to steal and too sorry to work. Steve was neither. I swear sometimes I would hire him to fix something so I could learn how to do it myself. When I didn't have any money or budget, he would fix it anyway just to have something to do and keep him out of trouble.

One cold and rainy November night, I saw him underneath the porch of the Church as I left. It must have been nine thirty and I could just barely see his shadow irregular around the corner of one of the buildings. "Steve, what are you doing here?" No answer. "You wet and cold?" Still no answer.

I eased him in through the boiler room door and said, "Please, don't tell anyone I let you in here." He was gone when I came back the next morning. I managed to leave the door open for a week or so knowing he would be back.

Steve was the child of an upper middle class family. They owned a liquor store and built high dollar homes. They made good money. Steve's father had the nerve to up and die while Steve was still a young man.

Steve could build a home faster, cheaper, better, and fancier than anyone around. He had money, women, and all the liquor you could drink. And, he did it all. He did it all for years, until it and he started to fall apart.

Neither he nor I knew when it happened. One day he just decided that nothing mattered any more.

He no longer enjoyed his work, and he no longer liked drinking. It was simply the place to hide.

You could see it coming like a freezing blizzard or a smothering snow. He showed up almost every day looking for work. His cough became consuming. Hearing the hack caused you to hurt all over. "It's pneumonia," he said. "I've been over to the Floyd Emergency Room. I've got some medicine. Can you help me with my prescription?"

That was the routine for over a year. He had been admitted to the hospital a couple of times. "Hey, Bill come visit me. I'm bored. Get me out of here." We must have done that a half dozen times in a year and a half.

Then one day he said it. I had heard it a few times before, sometimes from alcoholics, sometimes from the old, sometimes from long term cancer patients, occasionally from the depressed. "I'm dead tired. I'm gone. I'm gonna die." And, he meant it.

Whatever snatched his will to live from him, I do not know. Some called it alcohol, some called it addiction. Some said it was insanity. He was not ignorant about what was happening. Somewhere inside his soul he added up what he thought was ahead and decided it was useless.

I visited him every day. We had regular conversation like we always did. We both knew what was happening. A few days later he was sleeping all the time. They told me he had slipped into a coma. There was no more pain. Then one evening, just about sundown, the hospital called.

"Mr. Coker has listed you as the person to be notified. Are you a member of his family?"

"No Ma'am. I'm his friend."

"Mr. Coker is gone." I thought, Dead? Gone?

Why am I so possessed to pass this story on? Such is not unusual. It happens in every community in the world. It happens to nice people like Steve. But, I cannot help but believe that it was a waste. WHY? Somewhere in this process Steve became a friend, a close friend, family. If we believe that we are all bound together in this journey called life, attachments become the most valuable of all our possessions. Death is a robber.

Tapping

I hear you tapping at my window
      and I hesitate to turn around.
You have been here before
      traveling through our town.

Tall, dark, with vacant eyes and
      sun leathered skin.
You present your gaunt self
      time and again.

Got a dollar Mister?
      Got the time?
Tell me and I'll go away.
      Get me a room and I'll stay.

I hear the rustle of your arrival outside.
      I feel your loss of pride.
Perhaps Christ has come
      travelling through our town?

A Tribute to Tattoos

I see you sitting in the yard,
      you're back here again.
I know you're in trouble.
      It's written on your skin.
Tattoos are trouble.
      Mama said it's a sin.

Drunk tank disciple,
      brother of us all,
Midnight wander,
      sleeper in the hall,
Tattoos are trouble
      particularly when you call.

You said, "It's that woman
      that caused all this."
You paid for her tattoos.
      Heaven help Sis.
Tattoos are trouble and
      you are too, Miss.

Stranded in Tulsa
      waiting for the bus,
Give a call.
      He'll take care, without fuss.
Tattoos are trouble,
      Trailways is for us.

Call "collect."
      He's always at the phone.
Somewhere after midnight
      you'll find him home.

Tattoos are trouble
> when your money's gone.

Sitting in the Greyhound lobby
> You're still alone.

Whose Table Is This Anyway?

Whose table is this anyway?
    Nobody asked us to stay.
Thirty years we met here to break bread,
    surrounded now by the living and the dead.
Whose table is it anyway?

Teachers, preachers, plumbers, and pipefitters,
    carpenters, masons, and bull-sh***ers,
We all meet here with a story to tell,
    some of us fresh out of hell.
Whose table is it anyway?

Donnie, I can still see your eyes,
    Your heart has told endless lies
about your chances to stay.
    The sounds in your head play.
Whose table is it any way?

Jesus sat down with his men.
    It was supper time for them.
Sinners and saints they were all there
    Some would stay, members of A.A.,
    but not for the hour.
Whose table is it anyway?

Communion is confession of one's sins.
    Why don't you join in?

Strange

Too many stories slip away. I thought I would save a few just for my own laughs. Most of these memories come from small town Kentucky or from hanging around church.

Hoot

Recreation in some communities is limited to what the locals find exciting: drinking, gambling, knifing, and shooting.

In a panic, Hoot called my brother for legal advice. "I've shot a man and I need to turn myself in to the sheriff." Hoot's story included that he had been with a friend who was with another friend's wife when a drunken brawl broke out. Shots were fired.

Sam did as any good lawyer would, advised him to stay out of sight until a determination could be reached.

Three days later Hoot called in histrionics, declaring that he could no longer stay inside. He had to get out even if it meant he would go to jail. Sam offered him some relief. Apparently, the victim would not bring charges against Hoot. To cover up his own indiscretions, he had told his wife he accidentally shot himself. As long as the victim's story held, they would all be clear. Hoot could go to town.

Chester

In the greater unincorporated metropolitan area of Frog Level one could view some unusual activity if one was alert.

On a bright summer's morning I noticed a 1949 Chevrolet across both lanes of the narrow street. It was chained to a large oak tree. Periodically the car would lunge or jerk. Smoke would pour out of the rear wheels and great groaning and crying noises would come out from under the hood.

I watched for as long as I could stand and approached the driver's side to discover Chester, a local boy of some diminished capacity, I thought.

"Chester, what are you doing? That's an oak tree. You ain't never going to get it out of the ground like that." I was mistaken.

Chester's response was, "Get out of here boy, I'm straightening my bumper."

All is not as it appears in the universe.

Denver Dog

It was my second church in a small Tennessee community. I was one minister of three. Being Minister of Education/Administration, etc., means a variety of functions fall in your purview. For some reason it has always fallen my lot to deal with exceptional or unusual people with a variety of benevolent needs. There is apparently something about me that not only attracts such persons but betrays a kinship.

I have been a "pragmatic theologian." Practiced theology is the only true test of its validity. Some are turned off, others are frightened by the knowledge that all cannot be fixed.

However, the call was transferred to my office. The lady, with an educated tone, said, "Sir, I am ____, and stranded in your city at the Robert E. Lee Hotel."

My response as usual was, "How may I help you?"

"Well, I need something to eat." I replied that I could make arrangement for her to get a meal at the hotel restaurant. Her next statement caught me off guard. "Sir, I need a taxicab to Denver, Colorado." I fell silent, calculating that the trip would be well over a thousand miles. I offered her my best alternative, a bus ticket to Knoxville, approximately seventy miles north. Her response was immediate and firm. "No sir, I'm traveling with my dog. He's nervous and won't ride the bus." I told her I would call the hotel and get her a meal. She seemed somewhat disappointed.

Don't Look

Often individuals would appear at the Church Office hoping to get assistance of some kind. I would usually meet them at the receptionist's desk or in the foyer of the Office Building.

A middle adult lady of some girth had managed to get by the volunteer at the desk and presented herself in my doorway. "Hi, my name is Carole, and I need your help." "What can I do for you today?" I asked.

"I need some money. I've had surgery and have bills to pay."

"I'm sorry we don't pay bills. I can get you to someone who can help you."

"I'm desperate. Here, see my surgery." She lifted her dress, so I could see.

I screamed, "Stop that!" She did. I told her, "You can't do that here." She huffed and left.

Two days later she reappeared. I heard her plea again. She showed me her surgery again, and I promised her I would dial 911 and have her arrested. She left again

On Monday she returned and headed toward my office. She remembered what I had promised, promptly made a ninety-degree turn, and went to offend another minister.

Elevator

It was only a small freight elevator. We were unloading the weekly food delivery to Meals and More at First Christian Church. I know no good deed goes unpunished, but Cathy-Aiken Freeman, past director of Rome Action Ministries, and I were hoping to have an uneventful preparation of meals for the working poor.

Churches come each week giving of their blessings. When the weight of the delivery is heavy, we often use the small freight elevator to deliver food to the lower floor. Cathy and I entered the elevator with two boxes of food on the hand truck.

Cathy pushed the down button, and we were headed to the lower floor. About halfway down, we noticed a screeching noise and found ourselves halfway between floors in a suspended state. The nice gentleman outside waved at us through the window.

We tried the door locks and found them unresponsive. We began to laugh. We began to worry. I wondered where our faithful co-pastor, Horace Stewart, might be.

I called on my cell phone and received a cheery response.

"Horace, the elevator is stuck." I said.

There was a moment of silence and then an encouraging, "I'm on my way."

In a few moments he was on the first floor rattling the door, then on the second floor and finally on the basement floor. Nothing seemed to work.

"Do you have a key?" I asked.

"I don't think so."

"Do you know where the circuit breaker might be?"

"No." In a few moments, as we continued to laugh from the absurdity of the event, he let us know that the elevator people could be here on Monday. The elevator people were quite assuring.

We reminded ourselves that we had four hundred sandwiches to sustain us until their arrival.

I thought seriously about calling the Fire Department. That's what you're supposed to do. Then I thought about the newspaper photographers who listen to the scanner and follow. Indignity overcame that answer.

Now we are 40 minutes into the event. Cathy observed that the next floor up has a thumb latch. I suggested that I would climb up on the frame of the topless elevator. Cathy responded with "I can climb like a spider monkey."

I insisted on climbing up. It worked. The door sprung open. I found myself halfway on the floor and halfway on the top of the elevator.

One of the volunteers approached me as I lay on the floor. "I need those sandwiches. We have run out." It seemed less than appropriate at the moment. Horace came quickly with a ladder. Cathy climbed out. I climbed to the top with a box of peanut butter sandwiches on my head, and as I brought the second box up, I noticed Cathy taking pictures with her cell phone. Something seems less than dignified.

Somewhere later when we have stopped laughing, we will recount the event and laugh again.

Ham in Court

I swear this story is true.

Most adults have had the opportunity to do jury duty. I think it is a sacred obligation. Sometimes the case should have been settled. This one made it past the scrutiny of whoever makes such decisions.

On a summer morning, in the otherwise crime free community of Rome, Georgia, there appeared a case before the court. The defendant would not take the stand on the advice of her attorney. She had been detained by a local law officer at the check-out of a grocery.

The officer testified as did the cashier. The alert cashier had noticed something that seemed inappropriate as the lady, in a loose blouse and loose pants, sought to pay for a couple of items. Upon inquiry, a three-pound, six ounce, boneless ham was presented on the counter after being retrieved by the customer from her pants. Her explanation was, "I don't know how it got in there!" The witness was dismissed.

The District Attorney immediately rested his case.

The pro bono defense attorney, almost without hesitation, rested his case also. I desperately wanted to hear the defendant's explanation of how a ham might miraculously appear in one's pants.

The discussion in the jury room was filled with speculation.

"Maybe if it were five loaves and two fish, I might be able to understand."

"Perhaps someone placed it in her pants unbeknownst to her?"

"Could it have been in her pants when she put them on that morning and she just didn't notice?"

"Maybe she was bringing it back to the store?"

The verdict, unanimously, was "Guilty." I wonder if they serve ham in the Floyd County Jail.

Sisters

They lived in a purple house, drove a 1959 purple Mercury, and must have had 30 dogs who lived inside with them. In a small town they were quite a novelty, with their coal black hair and half an inch of stark white makeup.

But even more exceptional, they had built the only family mausoleum in our city cemetery. For two boys on bicycles, it was quite a treat for us to go to the mausoleum and look inside the windows. They had two rocking chairs, a radio, record player and a Christmas tree. It was rumored that they gathered there a couple of times a year to throw a party. We hoped that we might be able to crash that party, but no luck.

At the death of my Aunt Io, I got the rest of the history. We had gathered at the cemetery for the graveside service. It was only a stone's throw to the mausoleum. Aunt Io's son, Bill Ed, said I didn't know the whole story.

One of the girls, named Alaska, had a brother named Honolulu, who had died at birth.

I thought I had seen it all, but Bill Ed insisted that I go to Honolulu's grave site. The lesson was apparent. In order to keep her age from being disclosed, Alaska had gone to her brother's gravestone and had removed his birth date with a blunt object. Vanity is often at the source of our exceptional activities.

Real Law

Sam Davies was a high dollar lawyer, one of the best, nationally renowned. He entered the courtroom as quiet as a cat, well dressed, and professional in his demeanor. Cases were being assigned and today was "pro bono." It was "Rule Day" and all decisions would be handled by Judge Hopper.

Belowe shuffled in wearing the customary orange suit, handcuffs, and leg chains. She had only one arm with a tattoo saying, "Love only me" on the stump. The handcuff was attached to a waist chain. She was short, wide, tattooed liberally, and had a sullen and challenging look in her eyes.

Barbourville is a small hill town in eastern Kentucky, 2926 people with only occasional crime. There had been a wave of three holdups, done by a wide, tattooed, one armed woman. She drove what they called the "clown car." It was a 1957 Ford Fairlane 500. Every panel on the body had been replaced with another. Each replacement panel was of a different color. Thus a "clown car."

The first of three robberies in two days was at a local 7-11 in Boone Heights, done by her and a male friend. During this fiasco she wore panty hose stretched over her face. She plead not guilty for this one saying, "I had panty hose over my head and thus cannot be identified."

In the third incident she was caught and arrested for robbing a Quick store at Heidrick, two miles from the first. The "clown car," double barreled shotgun, and physical descriptions were identical.

"Mr. Davies, you have been assigned this case," Judge Hopper barked. "Would you please confer with your client and enter a plea?"

She mouths, "Not guilty."

Sam retorts, "Listen lady, they got you on video tape in all three places."

"It was a look-alike. I had nothing to do with it."

"Sit down, girl," Sam said. "I'm going to plead you to a lesser charge."

"Like hell you are."

Judge Hopper asked her "Can he represent you?"

She replies, "I want a real lawyer."

"Mr. Davies, you are dismissed." To this day Judge Hopper still says Sam is not a real lawyer. Belowe was convicted.

Naked and Dead

This story was not originally intended as something of humor. However, the more I heard the more I became convinced that it simply was beyond any reason. It was either an anomaly or sheer fraud.

She appeared in the outer office as a modestly dressed woman, impressing one that she was at least educated and able to express herself. She asked if she might speak to me about her father's passing and whether the church might be able to help her. The request seemed reasonable, and I escorted her to my office with expressions of concern for her loss.

"Daddy died and I need help with the funeral." I asked if she had someone to do the service, which is my usual first question, hoping to begin some process of order.

The question was altogether missed. "Could the Church pay for the funeral?" was the first inquiry. Before I could answer, she explained to me that there would be other expenses.

Her brother was currently a resident of an army stockade in Oklahoma, and he would need funds to travel home. We returned to the issue of funeral expenses. Apparently, the woman with whom Daddy had been living was not Daddy's wife, and she had absconded with the proceeds of the insurance funeral funds.

Now we turned to the major issue. All of them were in need of clothing for the funeral, particularly

Daddy. He was, in her words, "down there at the funeral home lying on that cold stainless-steel table naked." That seemed to me to be the most desperate of needs in this scenario. I had never been approached about the absence of clothing for the dead in 36 years of licensed ministry. Other questions became apparent: What happened to the clothes he had on at the point of his departure? Were they unacceptable by the family and discretely removed? Is there some legal standard for clothing the dead? What size is he anyway? Too many questions. She somehow sensed either my suspicion or inability to provide what she needed. She left muttering something about uncaring or unfeeling clergy. Naked and dead?

Names

It's all in a name, they say.
How in this world did your mama leave you like
this?

Ronnie, Donnie, Lavonnie,
Zonie, Donie, Omie and Onie
almost impossible to say.
All in one family, all in one place.

Your name could have been Rita,
but Uncle Ted named you Conchita.

Some of you came to the office door
with names to implore.
You said, "Sonshine, Handsome, and Curley,"
there were even two guys named Shirley.

What would you do with twins for a name?
Boys maybe Propane and Butane.
Twins for girls might be better with
Marietta or Alpharetta.

Two with a boy and a girl of the set
might be Bubba and Bubette.
Girls could be Nebraska or Alaska,
Men might find it difficult to ask her.

That's some and not all. It could be Biblical
like Tiglathpileser and Ashurbanapal.
Name it.

Norman

I can only show you what I have seen. Occasionally, in the ordered universe, one happens upon that which is out of order, that which does not fit into the logical scheme of things. They appeared out of nowhere, Norman and Mary Magdalene.

Norman had the detached visage of one long separated from reality. Norman's eyes did not focus. His hair had that strange look of being at odds with itself and had a very deep blue tint like that of an old Buick black enamel paint job that had not been waxed for a long time. He reminded one of a deep-fried lifestyle that had accumulated over decades. One must remember that Norman is just one letter from normal.

Mary Magdalene spoke with a clearer tone. Her left eye wandered as she stared at me. I found it difficult to focus, not knowing which eye was dominant. She had no doubt been taken by love into a relationship that was less than nurturing.

She told me I was there to tell him that he could not strike her. I had no difficulty with that. He had a clear intellectual understanding of the evils of violence. "Norman, did you hit your first wife?"

"Yes."

"Did you hit your kids?"

"Yes."

"Did you hit Mary?"

"No."

"Norman, have you been in jail?"

"Yes."

"Norman, would you like to go back to jail?"

"No."

Enough said. I told him I knew the judge and would have him put under the jail if he ever raised a hand to her again. He nodded his head in acknowledgement.

Two days later Norman could hardly resist the opportunity to strike Mary. He clearly remembered my admonishments. What do you do when you can't hit your wife? You go visit a friend who is equally as helpless. Friend, my eye. Push and shove him a couple of times and he'll hit you in the head with a skillet. This is no Mary Magdalene you are dealing with here. Off to the hospital to get sewed up, to the jail to get sobered up, and to the state mental hospital to get looked at.

Three days later they call me from the hospital. I'm the reason for one of their patients being admitted. "How did I do that?"

"Norman says you said he was a coward, and he had to prove that he was a man."

Occasionally I see him around town. Sometimes she comes by for advice. He seems to not be as advisable unless she is present. The last time I saw his blue-black head of hair was in the median of highway 411 on the way to Cartersville.

Pilgrim

Out of the corner of my eye, in the middle of prayer meeting, I saw her motion for me to follow. It meant someone needed help. There he stood beside Frank, brought here because this was where you bring the homeless.

Mama always warned me about the kind of company I kept. I learned about making friends from her—orphans, widows, aliens, homeless, and helpless. My friends won me no place in the social register. But they sure were fun. Only the poor really know how to laugh. Only they have no fear of losing it all.

The moment he opened his mouth I knew he was not from here.

"Where then?"

"New York."

Rounded face, dark hair, middle aged, unshaven, he reminded me of a line in Willie Nelson's song; *Shot-Gun Willie* "...your skin is tough as iron and your breath is as hard as kerosene." And yet, he had a kind of dignity of voice and manner that did not suit a homeless man. He started his story.

"Salvation Army's full." It always is, and many a man refused to stay in our "military style" respite.

"You say your name's Steve? What are you doing on the road?"

"I'm an electrician by trade."

"Want a job?"

"Not really. I'm on a pilgrimage."

"Pilgrimage? Oh yeah?"

"Seriously, Preacher. I'm a good Catholic. I'm walking from New York to Savannah, paying for my father's sins."

The only passage I could recall quickly on the subject was that "The father's sins are visited upon the children." It looked like that happened in his case.

"Well the best I can offer you is one night at the Honeymoon Arms, and breakfast. Frank will take you." I tell him.

Jesus kept bad company. The old blue haired bitties and white collared criminals of his community gave him hell. I confess that in my personal pilgrimage, I have not only kept, but sought out, some bad company. I have often wondered if Jesus presents himself in the form of Steve or some other "Red Headed Stranger" or pilgrim.

Resurrection

When Deacon Trulene, a senior citizen in her early seventies, shared with me that Lily had died, I had no reason to question it. Trulene knew most of our members and was early for the Wednesday night meal.

Lily was matron of a wonderful, loving and dysfunctional family. They were very talented but occasionally would have some internal family disagreements. They were not past sharing such with the church or with friends.

We all tried to be of help and willing to give a listening ear. That evening Deacon Trulene shared with the church during prayer meeting that Lily had died. We tried to contact the family, but we couldn't locate anyone.

"How did you know she died?" we asked Trulene.

"Her daughter Lula told me," she said.

I was making a routine trip to Walmart one afternoon some weeks later and saw Lily. I spoke to her. She was alive and at Wallmart! Resurrection? I tried not to let my astonishment show.

I inquired "How you been doin?" a common greeting in our small town.

"Oh, I've been fine. Lula's been telling people I'm dead. But, it ain't so."

I told her that I was glad to hear she was well.

My concern was how to break this to the church. Informal conversation seemed to be a better avenue than an announcement. Outside of scripture I have not seen a formal announcement of Resurrection.

Right or Wrong, Heaven or Hell

A calendar error resulted in an Elvis
impersonator and the Klan performing on the
courthouse lawn at the same time.

Right or wrong, heaven or hell
good or bad, who can tell?

Caught in traffic in a small town,
I made the mistake of windows down.

Noise, noise like I never heard,
screaming and music and hateful words.

People by the hundreds on the courthouse lawn,
some of them there since Saturday dawn.

Elvis on the left and Klan on the right.
Even for the locals it's a shocking sight.

Police everywhere armed to the teeth,
How long since we've seen such in the streets.

How will the Tribune or history recall
such a gathering so late in the fall.

Will this be a reunion or a cross burning?
Mind is busy and turning.

Who's the hero here in a small country town?
Is it Elvis or these hateful clowns?

I can't remember such a crowd.
I can't remember it being so loud.

Right or wrong, heaven or hell
good or bad, who can tell?

Slick

Everybody needs a "slick" story. Summer in Rome, Georgia, is like every other southern small town. Now more drought than ever remembered.

I was returning to my office. I turned on Fourth Avenue going north, took a left on east First Street, and turned toward the parking lot to my left behind the Church. Or at least that's what I thought I was doing.

The car would not steer. Instead of turning left, or going straight ahead, I found myself up on the curb. The impact was harder than I thought. The wheel on the driver's side went up on the curb with an unforgiving crunch. I had to get out and see what happened. Why would the steering fail?

I opened the door, steadied myself, and felt the pavement move under me. Well, it didn't move, my shoe soles refused to grip, and I was holding on to the moving door, trying to remain upright. The odor hit me.

I smelled chicken. What did that have to do with this? Everywhere I attempted to move on the pavement was slick as ice. It was obvious, the street was covered with chicken fat. Chicken fat.

Some trucker had taken a short cut through downtown. That was not appreciated. When he left the processing plant, he had failed to close the valve securely at the back of his tank, leaving us in Rome with two city blocks of chicken fat.

I laughed out loud. Took out my cell phone and dialed 911. We had an emergency. The practiced voice at the other end said, "Rome 911, What is the nature of your emergency?"

How do I phrase this? "Ma'am, I'm Bill Davies and we have two streets covered in chicken fat down here." There followed what writers call a "pregnant" pause. "Yes Mam. That's what I said. We have two streets covered in chicken fat down here, and shortly there will be cars going through the fronts of some of these stores."

Another pregnant pause. "I'll send an officer."

Shortly, a police car slid past where I was standing and an officer gingerly approached me.

The officer said, "She wasn't crazy, was she?"

Shortly more police and a large fire truck with hoses came and rinsed the street. We all went back to work. The wrecker towed my car away. I could hardly bear to ask my insurance agent if chicken fat was covered. Slick story? Maybe.

Made in the USA
Columbia, SC
28 April 2020